Content Development
Matthew Hampton

Artistic Director/ Content Development
Maria Hampton

Editorial/ Content Development
The Write Group

Printed in the United States of America.

For information contact:

Allen Entrepreneurial Institute
ATTN: BAMM!
3235 Evans Mill Road
Lithonia, GA 30038
www.aeiinternational.com

BaMM!

BUSINESS AND MONEY MATTERS

STUDENT WORKBOOK 1

Welcome

You have an opportunity to transform your life by following the Business and Money Matters (BAMM) movement.

BAMM is designed to help you design, start, and launch your own business. Research has shown that when young people have opportunities to understand how to start a business they become better employees even if they don't become entrepreneurs. The same research also tells us that entrepreneurial training can make your education more relevant and real.

We want to see you become a successful entrepreneur, but if this career isn't for you we want you to understand how to be a great team member in your future.

It is our hope that every young person in the world has an opportunity to understand the importance of entrepreneurship and the need that we have to build young entrepreneurs throughout the world.

If you would like to learn more about the BAMM Movement and the many other programs offered by the Allen Entrepreneurial Institute (AEI) please feel free to go to our website and learn more about our efforts to expand entrepreneurship in your community and around the world.

You are now part of the BAMM Network welcome and let's make it happen!

BAMM!

BUSINESS AND MONEY MATTERS

Learning Objectives

1. How entrepreneurs view problems differently than consumers

2. How to stay positive when you are faced with problems

3. How to solve everyday problems like an entrepreneur

1

PROBLEMS = OPPORTUNITIES

In this chapter we will learn the basics of entrepreneurship, how problems are the root of entrepreneurial opportunity and the steps that entrepreneurs take when problem solving. We will also aquire knowledge about some entrepreneurs who are solving problems in your community, as well as on a global basis.

When you master Level 1, you will be able to see problems like an entrepreneur.

Let's Make It Happen!

Entrepreneur's Lingo

As you prepare to become an entrepreneur there are a number of words and phrases that entrepreneurs will use and that you will see in your workbook.

Here are a few words that you will see in this workbook.
Let's review the words and learn what they mean!

ADVERTISING

BRANDING

BUSINESS PLAN

CAPITAL

CUSTOMERS

ENTREPRENEUR

EMPLOYEE

MANAGER

Entrepreneur's Lingo

ADVERTISING: a form of communication sent out by a business about a product or service

BRANDING: The name, symbol, or design used to identify your product

BUSINESS PLAN: A written document detailing a proposed venture, covering current status, expected needs, and projected results for the enterprise. It contains a thorough analysis of the product or service being offered, the market and competition, the marketing strategy, the operating plan, and the management as well as profit, balance sheet, and cash flow projections.

CAPITAL: Cash or goods used to generate income. For entrepreneurs, capital often refers to the funds and other assets invested in the business venture.

CUSTOMERS: people who buy the products and services companies offer

ENTREPRENEUR: A person who organizes, operates, and assumes the risk for a business venture.

EMPLOYEE: A person employed for wages or salary

MANAGER: a person responsible for controlling or administering all or part of a company or similar organization.

True or False

INSTRUCTIONS: Indicate whether the phrases below are true or false by circling your choice

A manager owns a business and makes a profit	True	False
Entrepreneurs are the last to get paid in a business	True	False
Advertising is publicity for your business	True	False
Branding allows you to keep your business secret from competitors	True	False
Entrepreneurs love discovering problems to solve	True	False
Entrepreneurs have to be negative when dealing with problems	True	False
A business plan will tell an entrepreneur how to network at an event	True	False
Entrepreneurs are paid to manage a group of people	True	False
Consumers and entrepreneurs view problems the same way	True	False
Capital is used to invest in a business	True	False
Entrepreneurs must be 21 years of age before they can make money	True	False
Global entrepreneurs do business in San Antonio and Dallas	True	False
Customers make investments into your business	True	False
There is a process to solving problems like an entrepreneur	True	False

QUOTE OF THE MOMENT

"When everything seems to be going against you, remember that the airplane takes off against the wind, not with it."

-Henry Ford

ENTREPRENEUR VS. EMPLOYEE

Entrepreneur		Employee
✓	Invests money to start the business	
	Is paid for hourly work or based on a set salary	✓
	Hired to manage and direct a team of people	✓
✓	Gets paid after all the bills and employees are paid	
	Has set hours	✓
✓	Is the Boss	
✓	Works more hours and harder than anyone else in the company	
✓	Is rewarded for taking risks	
✓	Can often times work all alone	
✓	Has no limitations on how much money he/she can make	

AALIYAH FISHER

Inspired by her great-grandmother Aleatha Racy, who was also a seamstress, designer Aaliyah Fisher has quite an impressive resume in only 4 years of being a designer. Aaliyah knew she wanted to design every since the tender age of 8 which is when she started sketching her own designs. At age 11 Aaliyah begin taking sewing classes, and needless to say that was the beginning of Grafetti Couture. At age 13 Aaliyah had her break in the fashion industry; she was selected by the founder of Little Rock Fashion Week to showcase her designs. She made history by becoming the youngest designer to ever showcase her line in any fashion week.

Fisher now 17 has been designing for 4 years and has showcased her line in several following shows, such as Mid-south Fashion Week, Mercedese Benz Fashion Week, New York Fashion Week, & Designer's Choice. Fisher has also earned recognition for her clothing line and by being presented with several awards. She was selected Designer of the Year in Little Rock Rep the Runway, Elevate's Youth Entrepreneur of the Year, awarded the Ivy Excellence award by the Chi Eta Omega Chapter of Alpha Kappa Alpha Sorority and 1st place in Battle of the Boutiques.

Fisher says this is just the beginning, she has big dreams of becoming a celebrity designer and opening her own boutiques to create custom designs.

STAY POSITIVE

ENTREPRENEURS

MUST ALWAYS STAY POSITIVE WHEN FACED WITH PROBLEMS AND WHEN ANALYZING THEM!

ENTREPRENEUR -OR- EMPLOYEE

Entrepreneurs are those who develop a business and assume the risks associated with operating that business. Managers and employees work for entrepreneurs. Let's see how well can determine who deals with each of the following business situations.

INSTRUCTIONS: Circle which best fits the given situations

Gets paid last	Entrepreneur	Employee/Manager
Invests money and time into a business	Entrepreneur	Employee/Manager
Receives a paycheck for their work activities	Entrepreneur	Employee/Manager
Hired to manage other employees	Entrepreneur	Employee/Manager
Takes a risk and expects to be rewarded for that risk	Entrepreneur	Employee/Manager
Works more than anyone in the business when starting up	Entrepreneur	Employee/Manager
Has a set time to come to work and leave work	Entrepreneur	Employee/Manager
Can lose money while working really hard	Entrepreneur	Employee/Manager
Takes out a loan to operate a business	Entrepreneur	Employee/Manager
Recruits capital from investors	Entrepreneur	Employee/Manager
Receives a salary or hourly wages for their work	Entrepreneur	Employee/Manager

HART MAIN

Man Can

Hart Main is a 17-year old that came up with the idea of manly scented candles when he was teasing his sister about the girly scented ones she was selling for a school fundraiser.

Although she didn't expect him to fully pursue the manly scented candles idea himself, he did, and the idea has turned into a nationwide success.

Main put in an initial investment of $100, his parents put in $200, and they all worked together to develop the candles as a group.

The available scents include: Campfire, Bacon, Sawdust, Fresh Cut Grass, Grandpa's Pipe and more. Today, ManCans candles are in over 60 stores across the country and have sold about 9,000 units.

YOUR THOUGHTS

Now that you know the difference between an entrepreneur and employee, let's discuss the *pros and cons* of being an employee or an entrepreneur.

INSTRUCTIONS: Answer the questions below using your view of you've learned

What are three benefits of being an entrepreneur?

1.____

2.____

3.____

What are three challenges entrepreneurs face when starting a business?

1.____

2.____

3.____

List three ways starting a business can change your life today.

1.____

2.____

3.____

Legends in Entrepreneurship

Birmingham entrepreneur and businessman A. G. Gaston (1892–1996), was one of the most successful African American business owners in Alabama.

Gaston overcame humble beginnings and racial discrimination to build a $40 million empire, which included a savings and loan bank, business college, construction company, motel, real estate business, burial insurance company, two cemeteries, and two radio stations.

Throughout the 1960s, Gaston was one of the richest black men in America, and was the leading employer of blacks in Alabama.

His motto was, "find a need and fill it."

A.G. GASTON

LIFE AS AN ENTREPRENEUR

PROS & CONS

THE FREEDOM TO BE INNOVATIVE AND CREATIVE

Young entrepreneurs love to be creative. Launching a business provides the opportunity to chase your goals and make your dreams become reality. When starting your own business, you have the power to bring your ideas to life. This is why so many young people are starting businesses.

IT'S EXCITING AND FUN

As a young entrepreneur you will have opportunities that other kids dream about. You can go into your community and make money. You may even have an opportunity to hire friends to work with you. If you promote your company the right way you could even be featured on your local news program. The world of youth entrepreneurship is filled with a number of exciting opportunities and fun experiences.

OWNING YOUR BUSINESS IS VERY REWARDING

At the end of the day, there's nothing more satisfying than knowing how far you've taken your business and watching it grow. Despite all the ups and downs, you will likely experience, having the satisfaction of building your business from the ground up can bring much joy to your career.

SOMETIMES YOU DON'T GET PAID

This is a tough reality that many young entrepreneurs don't want to face when it comes to starting their own business. Especially when your business is just taking off, it can be difficult to make ends meet. Sometimes when doing a project you can make a mistake in your pricing, hiring, or just miscalculate all of the expenses. When this happens you have to make sure to cover all of the expenses and sometimes you won't get paid.

YOU HAVE TO WEAR DIFFERENT HATS. ALL OF THEM.

Since you are the owner and founder of your startup, there are many challenges in creating your business plan and following it through. Your entrepreneurial spirit can only carry you so far through the struggles and stress of managing your own business. As the owner of your business, you have to be the accountant, janitor, and even the public relations manager. It can be stressful wearing so many hats.

IT'S LONELY AT THE START-UP

Being your own boss takes a lot of discipline and dedication. You have no one to rely on, but yourself as a small business owner. When you own a business, you can expect to work around the clock and spend much of your "free" time making sure tasks get accomplished and goals are met. While being a boss has its perks, it can also take away from your experiences as a teen.

CTE

DOUGHBOY'S YOUTH CATERING COMPANY

Q&A w/ DONALD "DOUGHBOY" STONE

DESCRIBE YOUR BUSINESS

Doughboy's Youth Catering Company provides catering services for corporate events, conferences, and private parties/individuals. We always work hard to exceed our customer's expectations because we're young

HOW DID YOU GET STARTED?

I entered into an Elevate Entrepreneurship Training Program. Initially me and my friends wanted to start a detail shop and that idea didn't get off the ground. Two years later I was in culinary arts and caught back up with Elevate. I figured that I could make a business out of my passion for cooking. Elevate awarded me an initial $300 in start-up money and helped me get my first couple of jobs.

DESCRIBE AN INSTANCE WHEN YOU FACED A PROBLEM AS AN ENTREPRENEUR AND HOW YOU RESPONDED.

My first event, I didn't get the food hot enough and it was time for me to serve it, so I popped chicken breast into the microwave, which made the food very chewy. After that event I worked even harder to make sure that I had two or three ways to insure that my food was fresh, hot, and of course not chewy.

I learned that as an entrepreneur you need help with small details that you just don't think about. I've messed up a lot more times than I'd like to admit but I have learned from each of my mistakes.

I also wish I had been a more serious student in high school, I now take my education very seriously and it's easier to be at the head of the class than to be at the bottom.

BEST MATCH

Let's have a classroom discussion on these terms and figure out what they really mean. Your teacher will lead the class in a conversation about each of the words in the entrepreneur's lingo.

Read the phrases below. Write the word that best matches with each phrase in the blank.

SENTENCE	BEST MATCH
I just paid the printer to create some new fliers for my company	___________________________________
I am crowdfunding $500 to start my new business	___________________________________
This written document has your marketing plan, operations, human resources and a financial plan	___________________________________
My aunt pays me to mow her lawn	___________________________________
I want to create a business that will help improve the appearance of my neighborhood	___________________________________
I am make sure that the other employees do their work	___________________________________
My friend and I are going to start selling phone cases together	___________________________________
I am having my t-shirts printed in Pakistan	___________________________________
I am going to pay my friends to help me launch my business	___________________________________
The swoosh on a Nike shoe is a part of the company's	___________________________________
I have developed a budget for the equipment I need for my business	___________________________________

SO MANY OPTIONS!

INSTRUCTIONS Choose the word or phrase that best fits each given scenario

1. What is the difference between an employee and an entrepreneur?
    a. A manager is an entrepreneur
    b. The car they drive
    c. Entrepreneurs get paid first
    d. The entrepreneur organizes and owns the business
    e. The manager owns the business

2. Advertising is best described as –
    a. Billboards
    b. Promotional fliers
    c. Television commercials
    d. Radio Ads
    e. All of the above

3. People who buy products and services from you are –
    a. Family
    b. Networking
    c. Mentors
    d. Investors
    e. Customers

4. When you meet a person who wants to help your business you are –
    a. Networking
    b. Financing
    c. Branding
    d. Crowd funding
    e. Advertising

So many options!

5. This helps people identify your company and it's product
    a. Branding
    b. Networking
    c. Consumer reviews
    d. Partnerships
    e. Business plan

6. The money that you use to invest in your business
    a. Capital
    b. Expenses
    c. Revenue
    d. Cost of Goods Sold
    e. Operating Expenses

7. Social entrepreneurs create businesses so they can
    a. Make a lot of money no matter how they impact the environment
    b. Buy a big house
    c. Buy a nice car
    d. Create products
    e. Solve social problems through their business

8. Which of these is a partnership
    a. I am hiring my little brother to help me run my business
    b. My friend and I are raising $100 a piece to start a new business
    c. My aunt is going to hire me to cut her lawn
    d. Meeting a mentor at a chamber of commerce meeting
    e. Telling my grandparents about my business

9. When an entrepreneur does business in more than one country they are engaged in
    a. Social entrepreneurship
    b. Creative entrepreneurship
    c. Global entrepreneurship
    d. Diagnostic testing
    e. Traveling to other countries

10. An entrepreneur hires this person to direct his team
    a. Business partner
    b. Family and friends
    c. Stock holder
    d. Manager
    e. All of the above

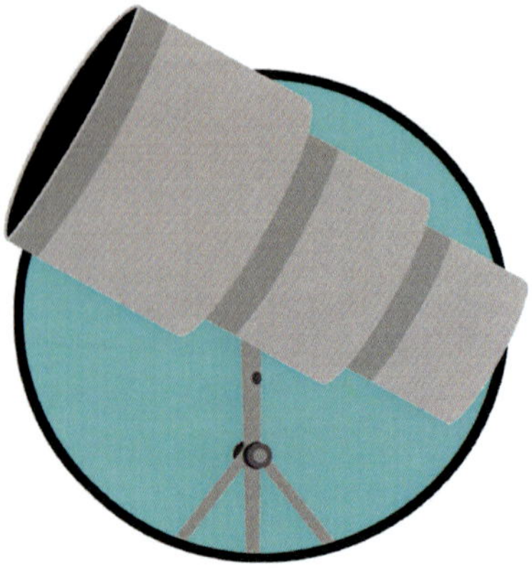

Specific problems that student entrepreneurs can solve, needs that the business can satisfy, and/or goals that the business can achieve.

CHANGES

Shifts in trends, behaviors, situations, circumstance, and/or laws, statutes, policies, and/or mandates.

INVENTIONS

Innovative ideas and inventions of brand new products and/or services.

COMPETITION

Understanding and responding to competition. For instance, underpricing the competition, choosing a more convenient location or enhancing product and/or service quality can help to generate and sustain a competitive advantage.

TECHNOLOGICAL ADVANCES

Engineers may likely be the ones who devise new technological breakthroughs, but it is the entrepreneur who decides how to use it and how to best sell it.

KIA'I TALLETT

For 11-year old Kia'i Tallett, living on a remote farm on the Big Island of Hawaii means you learn to make what you want to wear with your own hands.

"We like to make things instead of buy them," Kia'i told HuffPost of her family. Her parents, artist Sally Lundburg and surfboard shaper Keith Tallett, encourage their daughter's creative process.

Kia'i started knitting hats when she was five years old and eventually found herself with more hats than she knew what to do with. Her mom introduced her to Etsy, and Kia'i decided to open a shop to sell her creations.

Currently, Kia'i sells knitted cuffs and hats and felt flowers, but her resin rings are her biggest success to date, with a shop in Seattle, called Anima Mundi, placing a large order.

The unique, upcycled rings are made out of leftover resin from her dad's surfboard shaping. Kia'i selects the material from her dad's shop, he helps shape them, and together they sand them down until Kia'i is satisfied.

THE ROOT OF OPPORTUNITY

Building your own business can be natural for some young people, while others it can seem like a huge task. Entrepreneurs who can identify the source of a problem are better equipped to build a successful business.

LEVEL 1 QUIZ

Entrepreneur's Lingo

INSTRUCTIONS: Define the terms below

Advertising

Branding

Business Plan

Capital

Customer

Entrepreneur

Employee

Manager

Level 1 Quiz

1. Entrepreneurship is best described as
    a. Getting a grant to create a playground
    b. Making money for the things you want
    c. Organizing resources to support the development of a business enterprise
    d. Meeting people who can support the development of your business
    e. All of the above

2. The following are differences between an entrepreneur and manager except
    a. The entrepreneur owns the business
    b. The manager works for the entrepreneur
    c. The entrepreneur typically gets paid last and takes care of the bills and paying employees first
    d. The manager owns the business
    e. The manager directs a group of other employees for the entrepreneur

3. The following are the roots of entrepreneurial opportunity except
    a. Changes in technology
    b. Governmental changes
    c. Price changes
    d. Employee changes
    e. Competitive forces
    f. Problems

4. Entrepreneurs like problems because
    a. They can make money by solving problems for people
    b. They are mean people
    c. They create opportunities to network with other people
    d. They are symbols used to recognize a company
    e. They have money to solve all of their problems

5. Circle the words that are part of the process that entrepreneurs use to solve problems
    a. Identification of the problem
    b. Identify the market
    c. Networking
    d. Advertising
    e. Execute
    f. Strategic marketing

6. What problem did Dawn Dickson solve?
    a. Selling cheap shoes
    b. Women having sore toes
    c. Ankle health for women
    d. Curing cancer
    e. Hosting special events

Essay Questions

What are three pros of being an entrepreneur?

What are three cons of being an entrepreneur?

How do problems create entrepreneurial opportunity?

Challenge Question.

What is unique about a social entrepreneur?

Level 1 Quiz

NOTES

NOTES

2

VIEWING PROBLEMS ENTREPRENEURIALLY

Entrepreneurs view problems in a different light than consumers. Glass-half-full optimism is a key personality trait of successful entrepreneurs and that leads to seeing opportunities where others cannot.

For entrepreneurs, challenges trigger *outside-the-box* thinking!

When you complete Level 2 you will be able to understand and apply the concepts of viewing problems entrepreneurially, identifying opportunity within problems and see how other entrepreneurs created businesses through solving problems.

Entrepreneur's Lingo

Business Model

Expenses

Global Entrepreneurship

Networking

Partnership

Profit

Revenue

Social entrepreneur

Start-up costs

Entrepreneur's Lingo

BUSINESS MODEL: a design for the successful operation of a business, identifying revenue sources, customer base, products, and details of financing

EXPENSES: the cost required for something

GLOBAL ENTREPRENEURSHIP: The act of developing business enterprises on a worldwide basis

NETWORKING: establishing informal ties with people who can help a business grow

PARTNERSHIP: a business owned by two or more people

PROFIT: a financial gain, especially the difference between the amount earned and the amount spent in buying, operating, or producing something.

REVENUE: income, especially when of a company or organization and of a substantial nature

SOCIAL ENTREPRENEUR: Someone who recognizes a social problem and uses entrepreneurial principles to organize, create, and manage a venture to make social change. Social entrepreneurs often work through non-profit organization and citizen groups, but they may also work in the private or governmental sector. Many successful entrepreneurs, such as Bill Gates of Microsoft, have become social entrepreneurs.

START-UP COSTS: one-time only expenses that are paid to establish a business

Legends in Entrepeneurship

SARA BLAKELY

After attending Florida State University, Sara Blakely planned on becoming an attorney. But she faile the LSAT--twice. She took a brief job at Disney World, then sold fax machines door-to-door. While c the office supply company, Blakely had the idea for footless pantyhose that would smooth her figur and go seamlessly under white pants. She spent the next two years developing the invention, writin her own patent and cold calling hosiery manufacturers. Finally, she got a call from a manufacture whose daughters liked the idea.

She named the product Spanx. When she showed it to a representative of Neiman Marcus--by tryin on and demonstrating the power of Spanx in the bathroom--the representative agreed to stock Span in seven stores. In November 2000, Oprah Winfrey named Spanx one of her favorite things--onl then, when sales surged, did Blakely quit her job at the fax machine company. Blakely became th youngest self-made female billionaire, and in 2006 she launched The Sara Blakely Foundation to hel women through education and entrepreneurial training. Forbes lists Blakely as the 93rd most powerfu woman in the world.

MINDMAP

WHAT'S THE PROBLEM?

BONUS ACTIVITY!

Identify a problem in your community, school, or family.
Create a mindmap of different ways to solve this problem entrepreneurially.

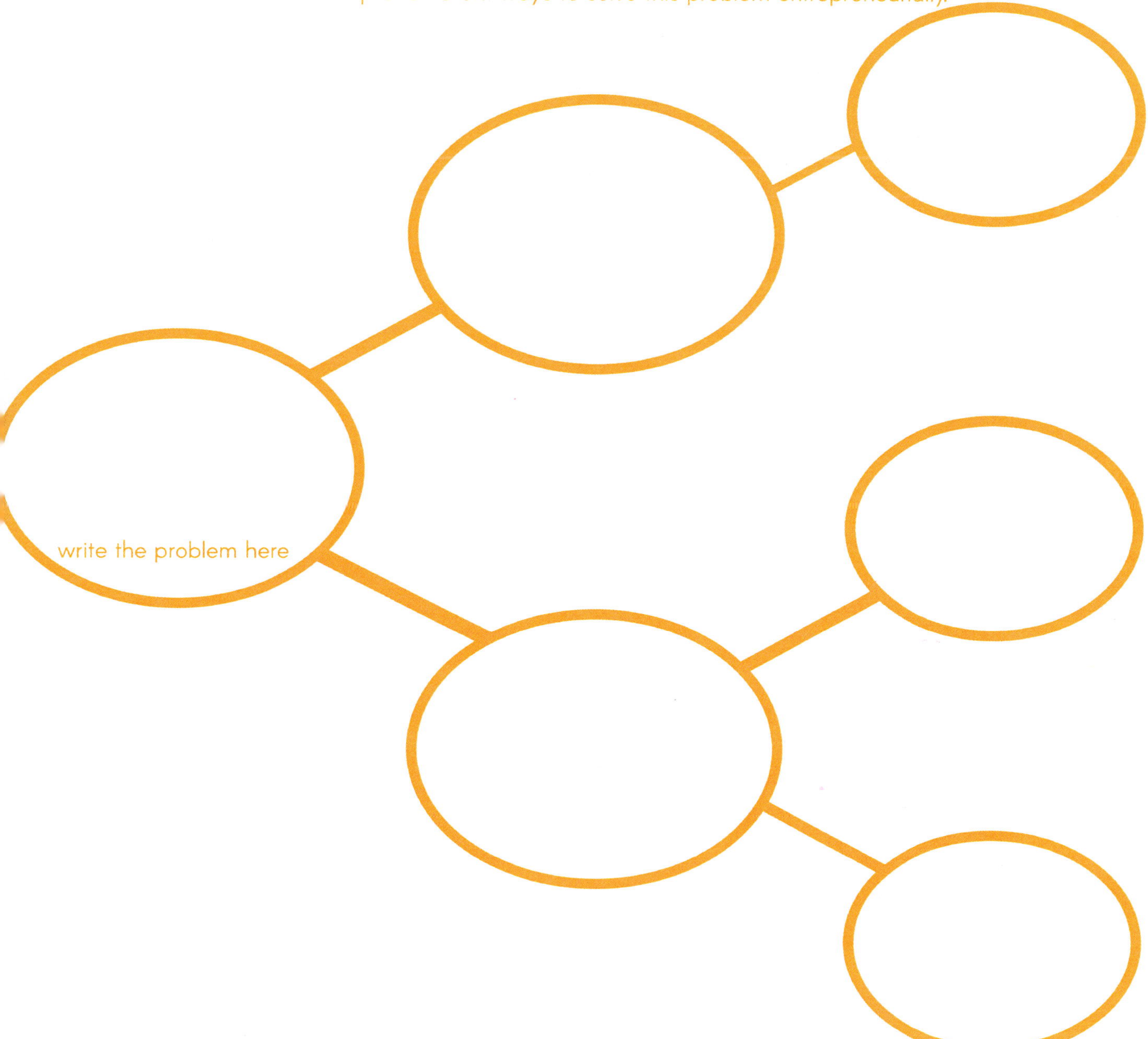

What would you be willing to work 80 hours for?

"ENTREPRENEURS
ARE WILLING TO WORK
80 HOURS
TO AVOID WORKING
40 HOURS"

Lori Greiner

CHASE REED

SNEAKERPAWN USA

Chase's passion for high-end sneakers runs as deep as his drive. Learning a lot from his father, Troy Reed, the oung entrepreneur turned his love for fashion and footwear into the world's first sneaker pawn shop. Prior o opening his business, he began reselling sneakers from his arsenal of more than 300 pairs of shoes. He even refurbished and redesigned shoes to make them look new.

Sometimes it would be a time when I didn't have enough money to buy sneakers or go out, so I would have to give my father a pair of my sneakers just so I could have money," said Chase. Giving his shoes to his father until e could repay the money gave him the idea that others would be willing to do the same for their coveted Air ordans. He carefully went through his prized collection and invested about $30,000 worth of kicks to create his dream. The shop sells new sneakers, designed by Chase along with matching hats and key chains to complement certain sneakers.

tarting this business wasn't easy for Chase. The self-proclaimed "sneakerhead" has sacrificed hanging out with is friends and many pairs of shoes already. He believes the tradeoff is worth it, however, especially with the relationship e builds with his international clientele. Reed says, "What's more fun than having your own business, seeing sneakers you've never seen before and interacting with people?"

Who Did It Best?

There are many companies in the world that solve the same problems.

They vary in many ways based on the main group of consumers that they serve (target market). It's important when solving a problem like an entrepreneur to consider what the needs of your customers may be. This enables you to offer a solution that best fits your target market.

INSTRUCTIONS:
In this activity your instructor will read different scenarios aloud to the class. You will cast your vote for who solved the problem best by circling the name of the company you select.

After the scenarios have been presented, a volunteer will tally all votes and the class will discuss who they voted for in each given scenario and why.

VIEWING PROBLEMS ENTREPRENEURIALLY

Scenario 1
You are running late for a birthday party and need grab a quick gift and card

Walmart Target CVS / Walgreens Macy's

Scenario 2
Your stylish uncle has a new apartment and wants to get some nice decorations for a great price

Target Walmart CVS / Walgreens Macy's

Scenario 3
Your five cousins are coming to stay a week for summer break. You need to get groceries, tissue, and soap

Target Walmart CVS/Walgreens Macy's

Scenario 4
Your big brother's 15-player baseball team just won a big game and they want to eat dinner together

Starbucks Pizza Hut McDonald's Red Lobster

Scenario 5
Your teacher is running short on time before school in the morning but is very hungry and must eat

Starbucks Pizza Hut McDonald's Red Lobster

Scenario 6
Grandma's turning 75 (35 if you ask her) and we're taking her out for dinner to celebrate

Starbucks Pizza Hut McDonald's Red Lobster

Scenario 7
I've been stuck at home, bored, and I really want to see the new big movie that came out today

Youtube Netflix Redbox Movie Theater

Scenario 8
The wi-fi is not working at home and you're having family movie night

Youtube Netflix Redbox Movie Theater

Scenario 9
Your best friend is sleeping over and you want to watch cartoon marathons until you fall asleep

Youtube Netflix Redbox Movie Theater

Scenario 10
Your favorite Aunt has broken her ankle and needs you stay with her until it heals. She lives 1200 miles away

Alamo (rental car) Greyhound (bus) American Airlines (airplane)

Scenario 11
Your sister's band is playing a concert in a city 3 hours away. None of them have a car

Alamo (rental car) Greyhound (bus) American Airlines (airplane)

Scenario 12
I want to visit friends who lives in another state but I don't have much money

Alamo (rental car) Greyhound (bus) American Airlines (airplane)

Tally The Votes!

Tally all the votes of your classmates below

Scenario	Walmart	Target	CVS/Walgreens	Macy's
1				
2				
3				

Winner! 1_____ 2_____ 3_____

Scenario	Starbucks	Pizza Hut	McDonald's	Red Lobster
4				
5				
6				

Winner! 4_____ 5_____ 6_____

Scenario	Youtube	Netflix	Redbox	Movie Theater
7				
8				
9				

Winner! 7_____ 8_____ 9_____

Scenario	Alamo (Rental Car)	Greyhound (Bus)	American Airlines (Airplane)
10			
11			
12			

Winner! 10_____ 11_____ 12_____

How many of your votes won? _____/12

MADDIE BRADSHAW

The Dallas-based company M3 Girl Designs was founded in 2006 by a 10 year old girl Maddie Bradshaw with a humble investment of $300. According to Maddie, She was passionate about art and designing creative things from the early age of 6.

At the age of 10, her passion took her to establishing a thriving company for young girls. In less than two years time, Maddie's flagship product the SNAP CAPS® turned M3 Girl Designs into popular national brand and she was selling over 50,000 necklaces and caps per month throughout the U.S. markets. Today, her designing caps can be found at various shops and boutiques across the United States, Canada, and the Bahamas and the United Kingdom.

According to Maddie, the inspiration of something like M3 Girl Designs stems from her family business of recycling plastic products. However, she was fascinated and initiated by her own idea and passion. She started the company from scratch and invested just $300. Besides being the founder, president, as well as the head designer, she is still a full-time student.

She is the member of swim team and likes to play lacrosse and tennis. Margot, her 12-year-old sister and great assistance in design, is the vice president of the company and attends business meetings. Her mother Diane Bradshaw is the CEO of the company and is responsible for all the financials.

I'VE MISSED MORE THAN 9000 SHOTS IN MY CAREER

I've lost almost 300 games. 26 times I've been trusted to take the game winning shot and missed. I've failed over and over and over again in my life and that is why I succeed.

–Michael Jordan

SO many OPTiONS!

INSTRUCTIONS

Select three items from the list below.

Use the tables provided to identify the problems that an entrepreneur could solve with these tools and describe the business that you would create by solving this problem.

Hammer	Dog Kennels	Water
Wrench	Canvases	Binoculars
Computer	Boat	Shipping Palettes
Paint Brush	Carpet Shampoo Machine	Tow Truck
Shoe Horn	Huge Speakers	Warehouse
Pressure Washer	Industrial Oven	Dirt
Coding Software	Gift Wrap	Open Land
Solar Panels	Sewing Machine	Plastic Storage Containers
Chef's Knife	Car Battery Charger	Laundry Supplies
Seeds	Bucket and Towel	Barbecue Grill

VIEWING PROBLEMS ENTREPRENEURIALLY

What is the problem that you can solve with this tool / product?	
Explain how your business would work	
Who is your competition?	
How you would improve on what the competition does already?	
Why would customers purchase your product or service vs. the competition?	
What other problems could you solve with this tool?	
On average how much would people pay you to fix this problem?	
Is your business a product based business or a service based business?	

What is the problem that you can solve with this tool / product?	
Explain how your business would work	
Who is your competition?	
How you would improve on what the competition does already?	
Why would customers purchase your product or service vs. the competition?	
What other problems could you solve with this tool?	
On average how much would people pay you to fix this problem?	
Is your business a product based business or a service based business?	

VIEWING PROBLEMS ENTREPRENEURIALLY

What is the problem that you can solve with this tool / product?	
Explain how your business would work	
Who is your competition?	
How you would improve on what the competition does already?	
Why would customers purchase your product or service vs. the competition?	
What other problems could you solve with this tool?	
On average how much would people pay you to fix this problem?	
Is your business a product based business or a service based business?	

What is the problem that you can solve with this tool / product?	
Explain how your business would work	
Who is your competition?	
How you would improve on what the competition does already?	
Why would customers purchase your product or service vs. the competition?	
What other problems could you solve with this tool?	
On average how much would people pay you to fix this problem?	
Is your business a product based business or a service based business?	

Legends in Entrepreneurship

Founded in 2000 as the brainchild of Nadine Ramos, LASIO® proudly holds the title of "keratin pioneer" in the United States due to Ms. Ramos' recognition of the unique reparative characteristics of this naturally created miracle protein, in an industry previously saturated with Japanese straighteners and harsh relaxers.

Since then, LASIO®, Inc has begun to flourish into a beauty conglomerate; introducing the world to HYPERSILK®, a miraculous line of keratin infused daily hair care products, and Keratin Tropic®, the first formaldehyde free keratin treatment. LASIO® continues to grow and excel as a brand committed to providing innovative products and tools for in salon services and at home use.

NADINE RAMOS

NOTES

ENTREPRENEUR'S SPOTLIGHT

Dawn Dickson

COMPANY NAME

WHAT CONSUMER PROBLEM DID THE ENTREPRENEUR IDENTIFY?

WHAT IS THE COMPANY'S CORE PRODUCT OR SERVICE?

WHAT IS THE COMPANY'S TARGET MARKET?

WHAT IS THE COMPANY'S UNIQUE SELLING PROPOSITION?

VINCENT KWOK

GINZENG

After nights of endless sleep in Deloitte auditing and passing all HKICPA exams, I quit my job before qualifying as a certified accountant. Why? Because I wanted to make a change, not only to my life but to everyone else's lives too. I the joined forces with two university colleagues and co-founded GinZengTM

GinZengTM is the first beverage with genuine American ginseng bites. We crafted the product so that it is convenie and accessible without compromising taste, quality and style. Aiming at reviving this ancient hero among young peopl we created GinZengTM with three main things in mind: "Keep it real, Keep it good, Keep it stylish

ow DO ENTREPRENEURS Turn PROBLEMS into OPPORTUNITY?

isten

he first thing you must do as an entrepreneur is to listen. Listen for problems.

.g. all the parents at the soccer game are hungry because the game was early and they didn't have time or breakfast?

Watch for Patterns

econd determine if there is a pattern that causes the problem. Are multiple people having the same roblem? Is there a time of day when the problem happens over and over again? What are the patterns or problems? Entrepreneurs must learn how to identify patterns to determine how to best solve problems.

nvestigate

fter you see a pattern investigate the problem. What are the root causes of the problem? Where are the eople who have this problem the most? Ask someone who has the problem to tell you how they would like solved. Determine if the problem is an entrepreneurial opportunity and what is the driving force behind e problem. Ask individuals who could be your potential customers to tell you how much they would pay or a solution to their problem? Ask them how they would like to see the problem solved? Ask 3 or 4 people nd if you see a pattern your almost there.

monetize

Now that you have listened to the problem, you've seen the patterns, and investigated the problem it's now ime to monetize the solution. Figure out how much you can reasonably charge to solve the problem. You lso must understand how much it's going to costs you to solve the problem and then determine the price hat you can charge for that service or product.

MAYA PENN

Maya has carried the title of CEO for six years. As a young child, she created her own clothing and accessories. When people began to ask her where she got her clothes, a spark was lit and the (then) 8-year-old created Maya's Ideas for others to be able to purchase the shirts, scarves, jewelry and hats she was making.

Her items are unique because all of her clothing and accessories are handmade and eco-friendly. Made with organic cotton, bamboo, hemp and other biodegradable materials, Maya has stayed true to the integrity of her company while expanding in the process.

Maya has control over everything within her company from creating the website to the company's brand extensions—an animated series and book are in the works. Business has been booming for the 14-year-old. Since she appeared on TEDx Youth, her international clientele has soared. Thus far, Maya has received the Black Enterprise Teenpreneur of the Year Award for 2013 and the SCLC Women's 33rd Annual Drum Major for Justice Award in the youth category.

Maya's Ideas also has a philanthropic aspect, with 10 percent of all proceeds going to global charities. Maya has also organized a nonprofit called Maya's Ideas 4 the Planet. Its mission is to help the community, spread environmental awareness and encourage girls to follow their dreams in nontraditional fields. "It's always been instilled in me, even at an early age, to give back and do good anywhere that you can," Maya said. "It's always been important to me to give back to the people as well as the planet."

photo and content courtesy of theroot.com

STRATEGIC THINKING

is defined as an individual's capacity for thinking–

CONCEPTUALLY,

IMAGINATIVELY,

SYSTEMATICALLY

AND

OPPORTUNISTICALLY

with regard to the attainment of

SUCCESS

in the future.

Level 2 QUIZ

Entrepreneur's Lingo

Instructions: Define the terms below

Business Model

Expenses

Global Entrepreneurship

Networking

Partnership

Profit

Revenue

Social entrepreneur

Start-up costs

Multiple Choice / Short Answer

5. Why is it important to listen to a customer or potential customer?
   A. To take advantage of them
   B. To understand their problems and how your company can help
   C. To get the latest gossip
   D. To engage in a great conversation

6. Explain why entrepreneurs need to see problems happen in patterns?

VIEWING PROBLEMS ENTREPRENEURIALLY

8. How did Dawn Dickson discover the problem that her company currently solves?

A. She read a book on entrepreneurship
B. She asked a lady if her feet hurt
C. She experienced the problem herself through her work
D. She met Oprah

9. How did Fredrick Hutson discover the problem that his company currently solves?

A. He went to prison
B. He went to Silicon Valley
C. He went to Dallas, TX.
D. He went to Africa

10. Identify the four steps that entrepreneurs use when problem solving

Step 1.__________________________

Step 2.__________________________

Step 3.__________________________

Step 4.__________________________

11. Explain the difference between the problem that the three following retailers solve for their customers

Walmart ___________________________________

Walgreens/CVS ___________________________________

Target ___________________________________